The
Tabernacle
of
David

The
Tabernacle
of
David

Written by **Goneey Kim**
Translated by **Janet Jun**

THE TABERNACLE OF DAVID
Kingdom of God 24/7 Worship

THE PURPOSE OF the Kingdom of God (KOG) Tabernacle is to restore 24/7 worship thereby re-establishing the Tabernacle of David. King David put up a dwelling place for the Lord so that He could be worshipped before the Ark of The Covenant, day and night. This place of worship, called the Tabernacle of David, is most important to be renewed in order for the Lord to reign as King of this world.

KOG Tabernacle of David is preparing a spiritual dwelling place for the soon-coming King Yeshua, in which the Kingdom of God can be manifested on the earth.

For more information, or to visit the KOG Tabernacle of David in Korea or the Tabernacle of David on Mt. Carmel, Israel please contact goneey@gmail.com +82-10-3080-7958.

TABLE of CONTENTS

---

1 Jesus' Hebrew name is Yeshua. This book uses His Hebrew name.

Let's Go to the Tabernacle of David

Let's Go to the Tabernacle of David

THE TABERNACLE OF David is not the Tabernacle of Moses. It is not the tent at Gibeon nor is it Solomon's Temple. The Tabernacle of David is not a house of prayer. It is not a church. The Tabernacle of David existed only once during a special period of time for a special purpose. And then it was dismantled.

But God will raise the Tabernacle of David once again. It will again be restored during a special period of time for a special purpose. And that time of restoration is now, during these last days.

> On that day I will raise up the tabernacle of David, which has fallen down, and repair its damages; I will raise up its ruins, and rebuild it as in the days of old (Amos 9:11, New King James Version).

It is only recorded that the Ark of the Covenant resided inside the Tabernacle of David. We know of no lampstand (menorah), no table for the Bread of Presence, no altar of incense. There was the ark. This tabernacle was a place of worship before the ark. It had no priesthood for sacrifices and no rituals. It existed exclusively for worshipping the Most High.

What a joyous journey it has been to discover, step by step, the Tabernacle of David! It is difficult to describe the depth of worship that began on the Feast of Trumpets in September of 2010, and the Tabernacle of David worship offered in that name after Pentecost in June of 2017. No matter how much worship is offered to our holy God, there is no such thing as enough. Each time we worship, God reveals to us the distinctive qualities of His character, and I am enthralled. Two years have passed since I wrote the book, "The Tabernacle of David". Now my desire, in this revised edition, is to share what I've learned over these past two years of worship in the Tabernacle of David.

It is the glory of God to conceal a matter, but the glory of kings is to search out a matter (Proverbs 25:2, New King James Version).

God oftentimes conceals His works, but He also gives us indications as to what He has planned. When we walk in obedience to God, it opens the way for Him to reveal His heart to us. Incrementally, we discovered more and more about the Tabernacle of David. And there was great joy in discovering and meditating on what He revealed.

As recently as ten years ago, our understanding of the Tabernacle of David was superficial at best. Since then, God has given us a glimpse of His profound Presence and of King David's passion. This came during times of intimate worship. Before this, we understood the Tabernacle of David as a house of prayer or as a reference to a restored sanctuary. However, God is now revealing a deeper understanding of the Tabernacle of David in many places all over the world to those who seek to follow Him.

On July 14, 2010, the Lord asked me, "Would you build a house for me in this city?". Following His command, a Tabernacle of

David was started as a house of prayer at the time of the Feast of Trumpets (Rosh Hashanah) in September of 2010. We were unclear as to exactly what He desired and so we began with a simple place to pray.

In these last ten years, we have experienced many trials and errors. Like children willing to experiment in the presence of their Father, we tried many things. In the midst of this, God directed us that worship should become central to our existence. In fact, that our lives should depend upon it. Sometimes, in yearly intervals, He would allow us to experience a joyous rejuvenation of our worship.

But in the beginning, everything seemed like an experiment. Our members couldn't play musical instruments. In time, they taught themselves to how to play and practiced until they reached a level of proficiency that enabled them to compose music and write songs. Now they are familiar with diverse genres and have composed, written, and arranged about 120 songs. When God put something on our hearts regarding worship, even if we didn't fully understand it, we would accept the challenge and make efforts to please Him. With a spirit of willingness to take on different challenges, we tried many different kinds of musical instruments: the traditional Korean *jing* (large gong), *kkwaenggari* (small gong), the traditional Korean drum (*jang-gu),* the shofar, the traditional Korean trumpet, the conch horn, the tambourine, and the tabor. Each of these instruments was integrated into our worship.

There were also many changes with the arrangement of our worship services. We made several attempts to form "Watchmen" teams consisting initially of one or two members and then five to six members. When more than 5 people were prohibited from gathering together due to the outbreak of the COVID 19 coronavirus in 2020, according to the Lord's former instructions to "build worship teams according to families", we were able to continue worshipping

24/7 even during the outbreak. With worship teams comprised of families, whether it was 2 people or more, it worked out perfectly. Just as Asaph, Heman, and Jeduthun worshipped as a team with their sons (1 Chronicles 25:2-6), God instructed us to make family worship teams composed of parents and their children.

> Of the sons of Asaph: Zaccur, Joseph, Nethaniah, and Asharelah, sons of Asaph, under the direction of Asaph, who prophesied under the direction of the king. **3** Of Jeduthun, the sons of Jeduthun: Gedaliah, Zeri, Jeshaiah, Shimei, Hashabiah, and Mattithiah, six, under the direction of their father Jeduthun, who prophesied with the lyre in thanksgiving and praise to the Lord. **4** Of Heman, the sons of Heman: Bukkiah, Mattaniah, Uzziel, Shebuel and Jerimoth, Hananiah, Hanani, Eliathah, Giddalti, and Romamti-ezer, Joshbekashah, Mallothi, Hothir, Mahazioth. **5** All these were the sons of Heman the king's seer, according to the promise of God to exalt him, for God had given Heman fourteen sons and three daughters. **6** They were all under the direction of their father in the music in the house of the Lord with cymbals, harps, and lyres for the service of the house of God. Asaph, Jeduthun, and Heman were under the order of the king (1 Chron. 25:2-6).

On the day of Pentecost in May of 2017, the Lord had us remove the name "House of Prayer" and instead take up the name "The Tabernacle of David." In December of 2017, during Hanukkah, the Lord showed me that the worship we were offering to Him was pleasing to Him, in spirit similar to the worship found in the Tabernacle of David. Furthermore, I felt in my heart that the Lord was saying, "It is not complete yet. You've just entered onto the threshold of the Tabernacle of David." At the Feast of Trumpets in 2018, He instructed us to build a Tabernacle of David on Mount Carmel in Israel. Accordingly, we began on Passover in 2019 to worship on Mount Carmel. We continue to give our all to worshipping the Lord at the Tabernacle of David.

Amos 9:11 says: "On that day I will raise up the tabernacle of David, which has fallen down, and repair its damages; I will raise up its ruins, and rebuild it as in the days of old." (NKJV)

There is no greater joy than to witness the restoration of the Tabernacle of David and to directly participate in its rebuilding.

This book is our attempt to share what God has shown us through our experiences on this journey. What you hold is the result of our childlike experimentations and ongoing revelations in this sublime endeavor. Our hope is that this can be an encouragement to others who are walking a similar path. An added blessing is that the more we share, the more deeply we understand the Tabernacle of David, which is something we greatly desire.

Shortly after publishing our first book in March of 2019, which dealt with our most basic understanding of the Tabernacle of David, we hoped to expand our offering by adding observations that have brought us into a deeper dimension of its reality.

The format of this book will lead you into the Tabernacle of David as you search the Scriptures and meditate on the Word at the beginning of each chapter. Elements that may have been unclear in the first edition have been simplified and chapters 8 and 9 have been added.

In the Tabernacle of David,
is only the ark of the covenant.

The Great Risk of the Tabernacle of David

Looking into
GOD'S WORD

Chapter 1: The Great Risk of the Tabernacle of David

1. When David tried to move the Ark of the Covenant the first time, he failed. What was the reason for this failure? What procedure did he use? (1 Chron. 13). The second time David tried to move the Ark of the Covenant, he succeeded. What was the reason for this success? What procedure did he use?(1 Chron.15).

2. What were the fundamental differences between the failure and subsequent success of moving the Ark? (1 Chron. 15:2, 12-15).

3. Read 1 Chronicles 25:1-31 and imagine the worship occurring daily in the Tabernacle of David.

4. Read 1 Chronicles 15:1-12; 16:1; 16:39-40. According to these passages, what is the appropriate place for the Ark of the Covenant?

5. According to 1 Chronicles 13:6, the Ark had resided in Kirjath-Jearim. Why did God allow David to place it in another location?

Now, let's continue this journey through the Word of God as it reveals the birth of the Tabernacle of David.

The Great Risk of the Tabernacle of David

DAVID SEEMED TO be off to a good start. He had conferred with his officials, including the generals and captains of his army, and also with the assembly of the Israelites. They had decided to move the Ark of the Covenant. Imagine how jubilant they must have been to have found the Ark and to have decided upon a place for it. They must have felt that they had everything perfectly prepared. They built a new cart and readied the oxen to move the Ark. The Levites placed the Ark on the new cart as they all celebrated, praising God, as the Ark moved forward to the sound of lyres, harps, tambourines, cymbals, and trumpets.

> So, David assembled all Israel from the Nile of Egypt to Lebo-Hamath, to bring the ark of God from Kiriath-Jearim. And they carried the ark of God on a new cart, from the house of Abinadab, and Uzzah and Ahio were driving the cart. David and all Israel were celebrating before God with all their might, with song and lyres, harps and tambourines and cymbals and trumpets (1 Chron. 13:5, 7-8).

However, a serious problem arose. When they arrived at the threshing floor of Chidon, the oxen began to jump and nearly tipped the Ark over. Worried that the Ark might fall, Uzzah put out his hand to steady it, but the moment he touched the Ark, he immediately died. Because of this, David became afraid. The Scripture recounts how David stopped moving the Ark and brought it into the home of Obed-Edom the Gittite.

Prior to this event, for approximately seventy years[2], the Ark of God had remained in relative obscurity at Kiriath-Jearim. However, after becoming king of the reunited kingdom of Israel, the Ark was located. Now, as head of state, David undertook to move the Ark, but failed miserably.

Three months later, David heard that God had blessed Obed-Edom and his household. During those intervening months, David understood and acknowledged why Uzzah had died. According to the law of God, only the Levites could carry the ark of God and it was to be carried on poles (Num. 4:15; 1 Chron. 15:2, 13).

> Then David said that no one but the Levites may carry the ark
> of God, for the LORD had chosen them to carry the ark of the
> LORD and to minister to him forever (1 Chron. 15:2).

So, David tried again. This time he had the Levites consecrate themselves and they carried the ark suspended on poles that were placed on their shoulders. A chorus of Levites, Israel's elders, officials and generals worshipped joyfully together as they brought up the Ark of God. David himself, danced and leapt before the Lord.

When they finally arrived at the City of David, they brought the Ark of the Covenant into the tent that David had prepared for it. This was the beginning of the Tabernacle of David.

---

2 The ark was at Kiriath-Jearim for 20 years during Samuel's time (1 Sam. 7:2), 40 years during King Saul's time, and when David became king of unified Israel and moved the ark, it was about 10 years. This totals about 70 years.

> David built houses for himself in the City of David. And he prepared a place for the ark of God and pitched a tent for it (1 Chron. 15:1).

> And they brought in the ark of God and set it inside the tent that David had pitched for it, and they offered burnt offerings and peace offerings before God (1 Chron. 16:1).

The Ark of God had been housed at Kirjath-Jearim while the Tabernacle was at the high place of Gibeon (1 Chron. 16:39). The Ark was to reside in the Tabernacle behind a curtain separating the holy place from the Holy of Holies, according to the instructions that God gave to Moses. The Ark was not an object that one could approach or gaze upon. Only once a year on Yom Kippur (the Day of Atonement) could the high priest enter the Holy of Holies to repent on behalf of the sins of Israel. This was the only time one could stand before of the Ark of the Covenant.

Now we see David placing the Ark in a tent which stood in the yard of his palace. There is no record in the Scriptures that a curtain was placed there to separate the holy place and the Holy of Holies of the Ark. In fact, the Scriptures are silent in regard to the arrangement within this tent. Yet without this information, we are still assured that God permitted David to move the Ark to this new location.

After David placed the Ark of God in the tent, he did something inconceivable. He bypassed the burning of the daily animal sacrifices before the tent of the Ark. Instead, the daily burnt offerings would continue at the high place at Gibeon (1 Chron. 16:39-40). David's preference was to have 4,000 Levites stand before the Lord, singing praises with musical instruments which David had made (1 Chron. 23:5). Moreover, he appointed 288 Levites to be trained as singers. The worshippers were divided into twenty-four groups, regardless of whether they were young or old, teacher or student, casting lots for their term of duty. Each team worshipped for one allotted portion of the day, and in total they worshipped twenty-four hours a day, every day (1 Chron. 25:8-31). Every team was comprised of twelve singers and 167 instrumentalists, worshipping night and day without ceasing, before the tent which housed the Ark of God.

Who could have imagined such a thing? David placed the Ark of God in the yard of his own palace instead of at the high place of Gibeon inside the Holy of Holies. A tent in the yard of his palace. And this tent God called the Tabernacle of David. God would not forget this tent, promising that He would one day rebuild it.

We are now witnessing the restoration of the Tabernacle of David which is being rebuilt all over the world. We give thanks to God for His faithfulness in keeping His promises. At the same time, the current re-establishment of the Tabernacle of David signals that there is a specific work that God desires to accomplish. He is seeking servants who will do as David did at the Tabernacle of David.

On that day I will raise up the tabernacle of David, which has fallen down, and repair its damages; I will raise up its ruins, and rebuild it as in the days of old (Amos 9:11, NKJV).

Visiting the Worship of the Tabernacle of David

Looking into
GOD'S WORD

Chapter 2: Visiting the Worship of the Tabernacle of David

1. Consider what kind of worship God desires.

2. Imagine visiting the sites of Gibeon and the Tabernacle of David where sacrifices and worship take place every day.

   a. Imagine the Tabernacle of David according to 1 Chronicles 16:4-6; 37-38 and 1 Chronicles 25.

      i. Imagine the worshippers: singers, musicians, gatekeepers.

      ii. Imagine the environment around the worshippers; the people, their expressions, the sounds, the manner and essence of the worship.

   b. Imagine the high place of Gibeon according to 1 Chronicles 16:39-40 and Exodus 29:38-42.

      i. Imagine what the worshippers bring and the role of the high priest.

      ii. Imagine the surrounding environment there: the animals, the sounds, the people and their expressions.

   c. Are either of these two places similar to our worship today? Why does God want to rebuild the Tabernacle of David?

Let's learn more about the Tabernacle of David.

Visiting the Worship of the Tabernacle of David

LET'S USE OUR imagination again to go into the place of worship, beginning with the Tabernacle at the high place of Gibeon.

The sights, sounds and scents of cows, sheep, goats and pigeons surround those approaching the Tabernacle. Crowds of people are bringing these animals to atone for their sins. Many are the offerings sacrificed to God here.

Drawing nearer to the Tabernacle, one sees the altar with fire which burns without ceasing and the smoke from the sacrifices being consumed upon it. Nearby, the offerings brought to atone for sins are slain. The Levite priests offer these sacrifices and other Levites are in attendance to assist. They present these animal sacrifices according to the law God gave to Moses. Then they wash their hands in the bronze laver and proceed into the holy place. Though onlookers can't see what is in the holy place, they can imagine. On the Table of the Bread of Presence is the sacred bread. The golden lampstand shines in the holy place as the fragrant smoke of incense silently rises from the golden altar. This is some of what one might experience at the high place of Gibeon.

These were the ministrations offered to God every day since the time of Moses. To the people of Israel, this was a familiar type of divine service that was in actuality a service to the individuals and to the community as well. The people confess their sins and present the priests with a sin offering or other variety of offering, (burnt, grain, peace, or guilt). The priest then proclaims their atonement and purifies them from their sin, putting them in right standing with the Lord.

> And he left Zadok the priest and his brothers the priests before the tabernacle of the Lord in the high place that was at Gibeon to offer burnt offerings to the Lord on the altar of burnt offering regularly morning and evening, to do all this is written in the Law of the Lord that he commanded Israel (1 Chron. 16:39-40).

Though there are differences in form between our worship today and the worship that was at Gibeon, there are also similarities. We enter into our places of worship with reconciliation in our hearts, as atonement has been completed through Jesus Christ. We come in peace with offerings of thanksgiving. As the priests received offerings and presented them to the Lord, our pastors lead us into praise and prayer to God. Upon the confession of one's sins, the forgiveness of sins is received. And after hearing God's Word and receiving a benediction, we return home with peace in our hearts.

Now we go to another place of worship. It's about half a day's journey through the mountains from the high place at Gibeon. The destination is Jerusalem, the City of David. Upon arriving, we hear sounds that we did not hear at the high place at Gibeon.

Is it possible that such a beautiful sound could exist on earth? It's the sound of melodious song and the harmonizing sounds of many and varied musical instruments. As we draw closer to the sound, we see almost 200 musicians playing their instruments together. Surrounding the instrumentalists, we see people singing and dancing to the music. Many others are sitting, watching and listening. Beyond the crowd, we see a singular tent that the musicians, singers, and dancers gaze upon. This is the Tabernacle of David. From where we stand, we can't see inside of the tent, but we conclude that the Ark of God must be located within. The praise of the singers is continuous. Surely their faces resemble those who are worshipping God in heaven.

> With them were Heman and Jeduthun and the rest of those chosen and expressly named to give thanks to the LORD, for his steadfast love endures forever. Heman and Jeduthun had trumpets and cymbals for the music and instruments for sacred song. The sons of Jeduthun were appointed to the gate (1 Chronicles 16:41-42).

After the allotted time passes, as the lead singer continues singing, the remaining singers are replaced by new singers, perhaps one or two at a time. Once all the members have been replaced with singers from the new team, a new atmosphere is present as the music of the new team begins. But the nature of the worship remains one of continual singing, music, dancing, prophesying, and bowing prostrate before God. This is the worship of the Tabernacle of David.

> David and the chiefs of the service also set apart for the service the   sons of Asaph, and of Heman, and of Jeduthun, who prophesied with lyres, with harps, and with cymbals... All these were the sons   of Heman the king's seer, according to the promise of God to exalt him, for God had given Heman fourteen sons and three daughters. They were all under the direction of their father in the music in the house of the LORD with cymbals, harps, and lyres for the service of the house of

God. Asaph, Jeduthun, and Heman were under the order of the king. The number of them along with their brothers, who were trained in singing to the LORD, all who were skillful, was 288. And they cast lots for their duties, small and great, teacher and pupil alike. The first lot fell for Asaph to Joseph; the second to Gedaliah, to him and his brothers and his sons, twelve… to the twenty-fourth, to Romamti-Ezer, his sons and his brothers, twelve (1 Chron. 25:1, 5-9, 31).

The worship of the Tabernacle of David is not comprised of daily offerings for the atonement of sins. Instead, it consisted of Levites dressed in holy garments, playing magnificently upon musical instruments to the Lord. There must have been awe on their faces as they worshipped before Almighty YHWH. And anyone who desired to participate in this worship was welcome to come to the Tabernacle of David and join the Levites in worship.

It isn't easy to find the quality of worship that existed in the Tabernacle of David in our regular worship services today. We can perhaps experience it during times of exceptional worship at one's house of prayer, or during special worship meetings. But imagine the worship at the Tabernacle of David as one singer began a song, singing and playing a musical instrument as the Holy Spirit led him. Sometimes the worshippers might have remained silent; it's possible that they might have danced or prostrated themselves; sometimes they might have played musical instruments without singing, and other times sang without instrumental accompaniment. The worshippers would not have been the focal point. They stood facing the tent that contained the Ark of God. The people were arranged so that the Ark was always the focus, and only the Most High was glorified at David's Tabernacle. God was present in this Tabernacle and the worship never ceased. Day and night the worship continued, and the smoke of the incense continued to rise.

On that day I will raise up the tabernacle of David, which has fallen down and repair its damages; I will raise up its ruins, and rebuild it as in the days of old (Am. 9:11).

The Tabernacle of David is now being restored in the nations. But why is God raising up Tabernacle of David worship at this time?

The House of God and Tabernacle Worship

Looking into
GOD'S WORD

Chapter 3: The House of God and Tabernacle Worship

1. When Jesus entered the Temple, he began to drive out the merchants; He turned over the tables and stalls of the moneychangers and those selling doves. He said, "My house shall be called a house of prayer for all nations…but you have made it a den of thieves" (Mk. 11:15-18, Is. 56:6-7). Consider what precipitated this event.

2. In Acts chapter 15, the gospel reached the Gentiles who were also able to become children of God through faith in Jesus. However, some Jews insisted that the Gentiles also needed to be circumcised in order to receive salvation (verses 1-11). To solve this problem, a council was convened in Jerusalem. Consider the decision of this council (verse 11).

3. After Peter shared his testimony regarding the salvation of the Gentiles, Paul and Barnabas testified about the signs and wonders among the Gentiles. After hearing their testimonies, James spoke regarding the Tabernacle of David. Consider the connection between the salvation of the Gentiles and the restoration of the Tabernacle of David (Acts 15:12-18).

It is time to restore the Tabernacle of David.

The House of God and Tabernacle Worship

A SHORT DISTANCE FROM the Tabernacle of David is Mount Moriah, the site of the threshing floor of Ornan. Later, King Solomon would build the Temple on this same site (2 Chron. 3:1). He would then move the Ark of the Covenant from Zion, the City of David, to the Temple (2 Chron. 5:2). The Lord Himself, with the Ark, would enter the Temple in Jerusalem, the city upon which God has written His name. As the Tabernacle of David was dismantled, the Lord entered the Temple in Jerusalem. The Tabernacle at Gibeon and the Tabernacle of David would now be joined together in Solomon's Temple in Jerusalem. At the dedication of the Temple, the glorious presence of the Lord filled it (2 Chron. 7:1).

Then Solomon began to build the house of the Lord in Jerusalem on Mount Moriah, where the Lord had appeared to David his father, at the place that David had appointed, on the threshing floor of Ornan the Jebusite (2 Chron. 3:1).

Then Solomon assembled the elders of Israel and all the heads of the tribes, the leaders of the fathers' houses of the people of Israel, in Jerusalem, to bring up the ark of the covenant of the Lord out of the city of David, which is Zion (2 Chron. 5:2).

As soon as Solomon finished his prayer, fire came down from heaven and consumed the burnt offering and the sacrifices, and the glory of the Lord filled the temple (2 Chron. 7:1).

Solomon's Temple might have united the worship of the Tabernacle of David and the Tabernacle of Moses. But as time passed, it seems that the focus became more on the offering of sacrifices than on the worship of the Tabernacle of David. For the daily offerings, the priests had to kill dozens (sometimes hundreds) of animals at the same time. Could it be that when they lacked the necessary workers, the Levite worshippers would be called upon to help with the sacrifices? We aren't told, but however it took place, it seems that the predominant activity of the Levites became the animal sacrifices rather than worship and praise. The singers would gather together again to sing at official ceremonies, but the daily 24-hour worship seems to have been supplanted by the daily sacrifices as we no longer read of the extraordinary worship of the singers and instrumentalists.

The sights and sounds that fill the Temple Mount become more comparable to those that filled the high place at Gibeon. And we no longer hear of the adoration, song, and music that once encompassed the Tabernacle of David.

A thousand years later, Yeshua, intimately aware of the worship of the Tabernacle of David, went into the Temple. The atmosphere filled His heart with zeal for His Father's house, so much so, that He drove out the merchants and overturned the tables of the moneychangers and the stalls of those selling doves. Then He declared, "Is it not written, 'My house shall be called a house of prayer for all the nations'?"

> And they came to Jerusalem. And he entered the temple and began to drive out those who sold and those who bought in the temple, and he overturned the tables of the money-changers and the seats of those who sold pigeons. And he would not

allow anyone to carry anything through the temple. And he was teaching them and saying to them, "Is it not written, 'My house shall be called a house of prayer for all the nations'? But you have made it a den of robbers!" (Mk. 11:15-17).

When Yeshua quoted, "My house shall be called a house of prayer for all nations," we might also understand this to mean, "My house shall be called a house of supplication, thanksgiving, intercession, praise and worship for all nations." The sacrifices offered at the Tabernacle and Temple were also forms of worship. Yet Yeshua fashioned and used the whip because those in the Temple had exchanged its appointed use as a house of prayer, and all that implies, for one of commerce. Where was the prayer offered to God in the beauty of holiness?

Between fifteen to twenty-five years after Yeshua ascended to heaven, a significant meeting was convened in Jerusalem due to a controversy among believers in Yeshua. Gentiles were receiving salvation through faith in Yeshua. However, some of Yeshua's Jewish followers believed that the Gentiles ought also to be circumcised like the Jews in order to be saved. The council of Jerusalem was formed to consider this issue. After lengthy debate, the apostles and the elders concluded that circumcision was not a prerequisite for salvation, but that salvation was secured through faith in Yeshua (Acts 15:6-17).

After hearing Peter's testimony, Barnabas and Paul shared their testimonies about the signs and wonders that God had done among the Gentiles. Satisfied by these reports, James broke the silence to reply and quoted the word of God which He spoke through His prophet Amos.

> "After this I will return, and I will rebuild the tabernacle of David, which has fallen down; I will rebuild its ruins, and I will set it up; so that the rest of mankind may seek the Lord, even all the Gentiles who are called by My name," says the Lord who does all these things (Acts 15:16-17, NKJV).

The apostle James then added, "we should not trouble those from among the Gentiles who are turning to God" (Acts 15:19). James connected the salvation of the Gentiles to the restoration of the fallen Tabernacle of David.

Salvation comes by the grace of Yeshua alone. He came in human form, and by His sacrificial death, He tore the curtain separating us from the Holy of Holies, opening for us the way to the Father (Heb. 10:19-20). Because He gave His own blood to cover our sins, there is nothing separating us from God and nothing preventing us from worshipping God in spirit and in truth. And since it was God who was bringing people from among the Gentiles to salvation, James said we should not make the way difficult for them.

Jews and Gentiles can now enter the Holy of Holies and both may worship as in the days of the Tabernacle of David (1 Chron. 16:28-29).

The Gentile believers in Antioch, in Jerusalem, and elsewhere, desired to worship God. Faith in Yeshua made each a temple within which the Holy Spirit would dwell. This temple has become a "house of prayer for all nations". Throughout the past two thousand years, God has provided salvation to the Gentiles, and in ever increasing numbers, Jews are now turning to Yeshua, their Messiah.

As James saw the Gentiles being saved, he brought the words of the prophet to mind, calling for the restoration of David's Tabernacle. Now is the time for the Gentiles to be, together with Jewish believers in Yeshua, that restored Tabernacle.

Heaven's Worship and the Tabernacle of David

Looking into
GOD'S WORD

Chapter 4: Heaven's Worship and the Tabernacle of David

1. David did not place the Ark of the Covenant in the Holy of Holies at Gibeon, he placed it inside a tent in his palace courtyard. The curtain required to separate the holy place in the Tabernacle of Moses from the Holy of Holies, along with the elaborate decorations there, are not recorded as being in the tent of David (1 Chron. 16:4-6, 37-40; Ex. 29:38-42). Consider what was unique about the Tabernacle of David.

2. When Moses built the Tabernacle and Solomon built the Temple, they each received the blueprints that they needed to complete each according to God's design (Ex. 25:8-9; 1 Chron. 28:11-12).

3. While it's possible that God had inspired David in its construction, we have no Scriptural evidence of blueprints for the Tabernacle of David. What we do have is the knowledge that David had a personal, intimate relationship with the Most High.

4. What God revealed to David may remain a mystery, but that He allowed the construction of the Tabernacle of David is irrefutable. Consider why God allowed David to erect this Tabernacle (Ps. 27:4; 1 Chron. 25:1-31; 1 Chron. 23:5).

The Tabernacle of David was a place of inspired worship.

Heaven's Worship and the Tabernacle of David

W HEN MOSES BUILT the Tabernacle, he had to make it according to the plans God showed him (Ex. 25:8-9). Furthermore, after the utensils and the items for the Tabernacle were made, God showed Moses where to place them. Moses could neither make nor place these items according to his own design, he had to follow the command of the Most High regarding every element of the Tabernacle. And the Ark of God could only be placed inside the Holy of Holies.

Uzzah died immediately upon reaching out and touching the Ark of God when he thought it was going to fall (1 Chron. 13:9-11). Nadab and Abihu died immediately when they offered unauthorized fire to God, something that He had not ordered them to do (Lev. 10:1-2). God did not allow anyone other than the Levites to move the Ark. And it could only be placed behind the veil. These were laws ordained by God. David placed the Ark of God in a different location, thereby violating the law of God. Yet God did not strike out against him, and instead, permitted it.

There are times when it appears that there has been a violation of God's law, when in fact God Himself, supersedes it. According to

Jewish thought, there is a higher law and a lower law. When the higher law and lower law come into conflict, the higher law takes priority. In other words, there are cases in which it is permissible to break the lower law in order to keep the higher law. For example, work is not permitted on the Sabbath. However, you may work if it's necessary to preserve or save a life. Saving a life (the higher law) supersedes keeping the Sabbath (the lower law), so one is still, in fact, keeping the law. Yeshua underscored this teaching by permitting His disciples to pick grain to eat on the Sabbath and by healing on the Sabbath (Matthew 12:1-13).

It's possible that at this point in His plan, God saw something higher in permitting David to place the Ark in a tent in his palace courtyard.

> One thing I have I asked of the LORD, that I will seek after: that I may dwell in the house of the LORD all the days of my life, to gaze upon the beauty of the LORD and to inquire in his temple (Ps. 27:4).

In 1 Chronicles 23:5 we read about the 4000 worshippers who were praising the Lord. The one thing David desired most in life was to behold the beauty of the Lord and to sing praises to ADONAI. While reading Amos 9:11, I realized that God wants to restore David's tabernacle, not Solomon's temple. It is my understanding that many of these 4000 worshippers were already actively involved in the Tabernacle of David and consequently, David selected Asaph, Heman, and Jeduthun along with many of these 4,000 Levites to continue worship 24 hours, day and night, with instruments he made for the purpose of singing praise. David also directed that there should be 288 trained singers from among the Levites. (1 Chron. 23:5, 25:7). This praise was being offered while the work on the house of ADONAI was being overseen.

Praise without ceasing.

Isaiah described the Holy of Holies in heaven like this:

> In the year that King Uzziah died I saw the Lord sitting upon a throne, high and lifted up; and the train of his robe filled the temple. Above him stood the seraphim. Each had six wings: with two he covered his face, and with two he covered his feet, and with two he flew. And one called to another and said:
>
> > 'Holy, holy, holy is the LORD of hosts; the whole earth is full of his glory!' (Is. 6:1-3).

The apostle John described the Holy of Holies in more detail:

> After this I looked, and behold, a door standing open in heaven! And the first voice, which I had heard speaking to me like a trumpet, said, 'Come up here, and I will show you what must take place after this.' At once I was in the Spirit, and behold, a throne stood in heaven, with one seated on the throne. And he who sat there had the appearance of jasper and carnelian, and around the throne was a rainbow that had the appearance of an emerald. Around the throne were twenty-four thrones, and seated on the thrones were twenty-four elders, clothed in white garments, with golden crowns on their heads. From the throne came flashes of lightning, and rumblings and peals of thunder, and before the throne were burning seven torches of fire, which are the seven spirits of God, and before the throne there was as it were a sea of glass, like crystal.
>
> And around the throne, on each side of the throne, are four living creatures, full of eyes in front and behind: the first living creature like a lion, the second living creature like an ox, the third living creature with the face of a man, and the fourth living creature like an eagle in flight. And the four

living creatures, each of them with six wings, are full of eyes all around and within, and day and night they never cease to say,

'Holy, holy, holy, is the Lord God Almighty, who was and is and is to come!'

And whenever the living creatures give glory and honor and thanks to him who is seated on the throne, who lives forever and ever, the twenty-four elders fall down before him who is seated on the throne and worship him who lives forever and ever. They cast their crowns before the throne, saying, 'Worthy are you, our Lord and God, to receive glory and honor and power, for you created all things, and by your will they existed and were created.'

…Then I looked, and I heard around the throne and the living creatures and the elders the voice of many angels, numbering myriads of myriads and thousands of thousands, saying with a loud voice,

'Worthy is the Lamb who was slain, to receive power and wealth and wisdom and might and honor and glory and blessing!' (Rev. 4; 5:11-12).

David's desire was to offer praise worthy of the One who is thrice holy, and to do it without end. And David understood God's desire to be among his people. David's desire met the desire of God, and the result was the Tabernacle of David.

The Key to Opening the Door of Jerusalem

Looking into
GOD'S WORD

Chapter 5: The Key to Opening the Door of Jerusalem

1. Read and consider the following:

    a. Psalm 132:1-8

    b. b. Psalm 132:13-14, 87:1-7

2. When David became king of a reunited Israel, he pursued a specific course of action. Read 2 Samuel 5:3-10 and 1 Chronicles 11:4-9 to discover what that course of action was.

3. Consider King David's reasons for capturing Jerusalem (2 Samuel 6:1-15, 1 Chronicles 13, and 1 Chronicles 15:1-16:6).

4. The key of David is connected to the restoration of the Tabernacle of David. Consider what door this key opens (Is. 22: 21-22, Rev. 3:7-12).

5. Consider the meaning of opening the door of Jerusalem in Zion (Ps. 2:6, Rev. 21:2).

The key of David can open the door of Jerusalem.

The Key to Opening the Door of Jerusalem

DAVID EARNESTLY DESIRED a dwelling place for the Ark of God and for the LORD, vowing:

> I will not enter my house or get into my bed, I will not give sleep to my eyes or slumber to my eyelids, until I find a place for the LORD, a dwelling place for the Mighty One of Jacob.
>
> Behold, we heard of it in Ephrathah; we found it in the fields of Jaar.
>
> Let us go to his dwelling place; let us worship at his footstool!
>
> Arise, O LORD, and go to your resting place, you and the ark of your might (Ps. 132:3-8).

After regaining possession of the Ark of God from Kiriath-Jearim, David was eager to find a worthy place for the Ark of God. He might have chosen Gilgal or Shiloh, where the Ark had been kept since the time of Joshua, or perhaps Bethel, Shechem, or Hebron, all of great significance to his forefathers. But it seems, in the end, he knew the place chosen by God.

For the LORD has chosen Zion; he has desired it for his dwelling place:

> 'This is my resting place forever; here I will dwell, for I have desired it.'
>
> (Ps. 132:13-14).

> On the holy mount stands the city he founded; the LORD loves the gates of Zion more than all the dwelling places of Jacob. And of Zion it shall be said, 'This one and that one were born in her'; for the Most High himself will establish her (Ps. 87:1-2, 5).

He said, 'Take your son, your only son Isaac, whom you love, and go to the land of Moriah, and offer him there as a burnt offering on one of the mountains of which I shall tell you.' (Gen. 22:2).

This was the place, Jerusalem, where the Jebusites lived. One of David's first initiatives after becoming king of the reunited tribes of Israel and Judah was to capture Jerusalem (2 Sam. 5:3-7). He fought against the Jebusites and prevailed, capturing their stronghold. The name of that fortress was Zion. He took possession of their city and called it the City of David. It was also known as the stronghold of Zion and Jerusalem. This is the place of which it is written that God would dwell there forever.

David had recovered the Ark of God and captured the stronghold of Zion where the Ark would reside. Then he moved the Ark of God to Zion, the City of David. However, since there was as yet no temple there, the tent was erected as a temporary home for the Ark of the Covenant. David desired to build the Temple (2 Sam. 7:1-3), but God did not allow it, and the Ark of God stayed in this tent for at least thirty-three years under David's reign. According to the Scriptures, there is something about this Tabernacle of David that God desires to restore.

For those who wish to participate in the restoration of David's

Tabernacle, two things must be found: The first is the Ark of God, the place of His presence and the seat of His throne on earth. And the second, is a location for it.

> After the death of King David, the rulers and the people of Israel became corrupt. Consequently, the Temple could no longer house the Holy of Holies on earth. God would not dwell in the midst of idolatry. Because of this, Solomon's Temple was destroyed by Israel's enemies. It was later rebuilt but again it was destroyed. However, God said that someday, someone like David would appear and rebuild it once more.

> And I will place on his shoulder the key of the house of David. He shall open, and none shall shut; and he shall shut, and none shall open. And I will fasten him like a peg in a secure place, and he will become a throne of honor to his father's house (Isaiah 22:22-23).

> In those days and at that time I will cause a righteous Branch to spring up for David, and he shall execute justice and righteousness in the land (Jeremiah 33:15).

> My servant David shall be king over them, and they shall all have one shepherd. They shall walk in my rules and be careful to obey my statutes. They shall dwell in the land that I gave to my servant Jacob, where your fathers lived. They and their children and their children's children shall dwell there forever, and David my servant shall be their prince forever (Ez. 37:24-25).

What does it mean to have the key of David that opens doors no one can shut, and shuts doors no one can open? The key of David is associated with God's Kingdom on earth. Might it be to open doors as David did with the Tabernacle of David?

It is Yeshua who holds the keys of David. When Yeshua returns, He will open the door to the New Jerusalem that comes down from heaven, in which resides the throne room and the presence of God.

As for me, I have set my King on Zion, my holy hill (Ps. 2:6).

The Key to Welcoming the Kingdom of God

Looking into
GOD'S WORD

Chapter 6: The Key to Welcoming the Kingdom of God

1. Consider the most important aspects of God's kingdom.

2. After David became king and reunited the twelve tribes of Israel, he captured the stronghold of Zion and brought the Ark of the Covenant there. Consider David's priorities in the establishing of God's kingdom on earth. (Ps. 10:16, 24:7-10, 68:24, 97:1, 145:1)

3. Consider the function of the Tabernacle of David in God's kingdom.

4. Consider what the connection might be between, "On that day I will restore the fallen tabernacle of David" (Amos 9:11), and "Your kingdom come" (Matthew 6:10).

5. Consider what must be established in order to welcome the King (Zech. 14:9, Is. 52:7, Rev. 19:11-16).

The Function of the Tabernacle of David is to welcome the heavenly King.

The Key to Welcoming the Kingdom of God

OCCASIONALLY ONE WILL hear the words "country" and "kingdom" used interchangeably. However, the definition of kingdom is, "A country, state, or territory ruled by a king or queen". England is called the "United Kingdom" because Queen Elizabeth II owns the superior interest of all the land in England, Wales, and Northern Ireland. And should her kingdom conquer another and annex that land to her kingdom, the queen would then own and rule that land as well. A kingdom is defined by the uncontestable sovereignty of its king or queen owing to his or her ownership of the territory.

A king may appoint a subordinate ruler to govern the population of a region that the king owns. In this case, the king would become the king of kings. In the Scriptures, it is written that God is "the blessed and only Sovereign, the King of kings and the Lord of lords" (1 Tim. 6:15).

He is the KING OF KINGS, AND LORD OF LORDS (Rev. 19:16).

And the LORD will be king over all the earth. On that day the LORD will be one and his name one (Zech. 14:9).

The political structure and function of a kingdom is determined by this concept of kingship. If a governing assembly of the kingdom is given more power than the king, then the country becomes one that is ruled by assembly. If the citizens have more power than the king, then the country becomes one that is ruled by its citizenry. If political parties have more power than the king, then it is the political parties that actually control the kingdom.

But in the Scriptures, we see that David had a clear understanding of kingship. When David was chosen to be king, he seemed to recognize that although God had appointed and anointed him as ruler over Israel, the true King was the Lord God Almighty.

Consider what Solomon declared before the living God when he sacrificed a thousand burnt offerings.

> O LORD God, let your word to David my father be now fulfilled, for you have made me king over a people as numerous as the dust of the earth. Give me now wisdom and knowledge to go out and come in before this people, for who can govern this people of yours, which is so great? (2 Chron. 1:9-10).

As king, Solomon asked God for the wisdom and knowledge to be able to govern the people of Israel (1 Kings 3:9). Because God was pleased with his choice, Solomon received not only wisdom and knowledge but also riches and honor. However, when he asked for wisdom, he believed that he was king. In the depths of his heart, he didn't wholly enthrone God as the absolute king. And in the end, he made himself higher than God, forsaking obedience to the One who is high and over all.

> For when Solomon was old, his wives turned away his heart after other gods, and his heart was not wholly true to the LORD his God, as was the heart of David his father. For Solomon went

after Ashtoreth the goddess of the Sidonians, and after Milcom
the abomination of the Ammonites (1 Kings 11:4-5).

In contrast, King David's declaration was quite different. In the
depths of David's heart, God Almighty was the only sovereign king.
This perspective remained until the day he died.

> The LORD is king forever and ever; the nations perish from
> his land (Ps. 10:16).

> Who is this King of glory? The LORD of hosts, he is the King
> of glory! Selah (Ps. 24:10).

> I will extol you, my God and King, and bless your name for-
> ever and ever. Your kingdom is an everlasting kingdom, and
> your dominion endures throughout all generations. The
> LORD is faithful in all his words and kind in all his works
> (Ps. 145:1, 13).

Furthermore, David had only one desire. He wanted to serve the
everlasting Lord and be guided by Him alone; to live serving Him
as King and gazing upon His beauty.

> One thing have I asked of the LORD, that will I seek after:

> that I may dwell in the house of the LORD all the days of my
> life, to gaze upon the beauty of the LORD and to inquire in
> his temple (Ps. 27:4).

David's yearning was to live in a kingdom governed by God. He
maintained that it would be enough just to be a guard in the Temple
of the Lord. And he wanted to pass on the everlasting kingdom to
his descendants. Because of this, when he became king, David built
the Tabernacle of David and brought the Ark of the Covenant to
Mount Zion to reside there. In order for the Kingdom of God to

be made manifest, the King must be there. The kingdom of God is where the Lord God reigns and rules as King.

On that day, ADONAI will be King of kings and Lord of lords over the whole world (Zech. 14:9, Is. 52:7, Rev. 19:11-16). The Kingdom will come (Matt. 6:10). The Tabernacle of David was a foreshadowing of the worship of King Yeshua. This is why the Tabernacle of David must be restored.

> In that day I will raise up the booth of David that is fallen and repair its breaches, and raise up its ruins and rebuild it as in the days of old (Amos 9:11, NKJV).

> Your procession is seen, O God, the procession of my God, my King, into the sanctuary (Ps. 68:24).

Opening the King's Highway

Looking into
GOD'S WORD

Chapter 7: Opening the King's Highway

1. In the last days when King Yeshua comes in glory to reign on earth, the prophesies regarding His return will all be fulfilled. As the day approaches, we can participate by our obedience to Him.

   a. How will the Gospel be spread? (Acts 1:8, Matt. 24:14)

   b. When revival comes, what changes will take place in Israel?
   (Is. 11:12, 15-16; Rom. 11:11-12, 25-26; Ez. 37:15-28)

   c. What developments will simultaneously occur among both Jewish congregations and Gentile churches? (Eph. 2:13-22)

2. The manifestation of the One New Man will precede the coming of Yeshua in the last days. How will Shem, Ham and Japheth become united? (Gen. 9:26- 27)
   How will "the remnant of Edom and the nations called by my name" become the Lord's inheritance? (Amos 9:11-12)

3. Where will God release the above events?

The Tabernacle of David will be headquarters in the last days.

Chapter 7

Opening the King's Highway

W HEN PEOPLE FIRST hear about the end of this age, they're often afraid. They fear earthquakes, wars, the mark of the beast, persecution, and other severe circumstances. When Yeshua spoke of the signs of the end times, he taught that there would be tribulations followed by judgment (Matt. 24:3-31).

However, if we look at these signs as preceding the coming of the Kingdom of God, we have hope. Irvin Baxter remarked of the end times that "It is the end of this world's government and the start of God's government."[3]

When the world's governmental systems come to an end, God's Kingdom will reign on earth. Therefore, rather than being afraid, we should be joyful that the government and rule of God will begin. We will enter His Kingdom, which has been our heart's desire. But in the last days, before God's government is established, there are several things of which He spoke that must first be fulfilled.

First, the Gospel of heaven must reach to the ends of the earth.

---

3 Irvin Baxter Jr, "Evidence That Now Is the End of The Age," Brad TV, May 9, 2018, video, 36:25, https://youtu.be/Jxho9UCWUzE

> But you will receive power when the Holy Spirit has come upon you, and you will be my witnesses in Jerusalem and in all Judea and Samaria, and to the end of the earth (Acts 1:8).

> And this gospel of the kingdom will be proclaimed throughout the whole world as a testimony to all nations, and then the end will come (Matt. 24:14).

Presently, the gospel is being brought to unreached people groups throughout the world. Furthermore, the Scriptures indicate that a time will come when the Holy Spirit will be poured out upon all mankind, accompanied with great signs and wonders that the whole world will see. And "At that time, whoever calls on the name of the LORD will be saved" (Joel 2:28- 32).

Second, Israel will be restored. Not only does this mean the rebirth of the nation of Israel, but it also includes the return of the Jewish people scattered among all the nations, something that will surpass the Exodus from Egypt.

> And the LORD will utterly destroy the tongue of the Sea of Egypt, and will wave his hand over the River with his scorching breath, and strike it into seven channels, and he will lead people across in sandals. And there will be a highway from Assyria for the remnant that remains of his people, as there was for Israel when they came up from the land of Egypt (Is. 11:15-16).

> Therefore, behold, the days are coming, declares the LORD, when it shall no longer be said, 'As the LORD lives who brought up the people of Israel out of the land of Egypt,' but 'As the LORD lives who brought up the people of Israel out of the north country and out of all the countries where he had driven them.' For I will bring them back to their own land that I gave to their fathers (Jer. 16:14-15).

The failure of the nation of Israel to recognize their Messiah over 2,000 years ago, does not suggest that God has deserted them. God has given Gentiles the opportunity to be saved until the complete number of Gentiles comes to salvation. However, in the last days, all Israel will be saved.

> So, I ask, did they stumble in order that they might fall? By no means! Rather, through their trespass salvation has come to the Gentiles, so as to make Israel jealous. Now if their trespass means riches for the world, and if their failure means riches for the Gentiles, how much more will their full inclusion mean! (Romans 11:11-12).

> Lest you be wise in your own sight, I do not want you to be unaware of this mystery, brothers: a partial hardening has come upon Israel, until the fullness of the Gentiles has come in. And in this way all Israel will be saved, as it is written, 'The Deliverer will come from Zion, he will banish ungodliness from Jacob' (Romans 11:25-26).

In the end of days, Judah and Israel will be reunited. Israel will be restored. And God's Temple will be in Israel.

> …then say to them, thus says the Lord GOD: 'Behold, I will take the people of Israel from the nations among which they have gone, and will gather them from all around, and bring them to their own land. And I will make them one nation in the land, on the mountains of Israel. And one king shall be king over them all, and they shall be no longer two nations, and no longer divided into two kingdoms…I will make a covenant of peace with them. It shall be an everlasting covenant with them. And I will set them in their land and multiply them, and will set my sanctuary in their midst forevermore. My dwelling place shall be with them, and I will be their God,

and they shall be my people. Then the nations will know that I am the LORD who sanctifies Israel, when my sanctuary is in their midst forevermore' (Ez. 37:21-22, 27-28).

Third, restored Israel and those who believe from among the Gentiles will become One New Man. We know this work will be accomplished because the One New Man will be God's dwelling place.

But now in Christ Jesus you who once were far off have been brought near by the blood of Christ. For he himself is our peace, who has made us both one and has broken down in his flesh the dividing wall of hostility by abolishing the [enmity occasioned by the] law of commandments expressed in ordinances that he might create in himself one new man in place of the two, so making peace, and might reconcile us both to God in one body through the cross, thereby killing the hostility. And he came and preached peace to you who were far off and peace to those who were near. For through him we both have access in one Spirit to the Father. So, then you are no longer strangers and aliens, but you are fellow citizens with the saints and members of the household of God, built on the foundation of the apostles and prophets, Christ Jesus himself being the corner-stone, in whom the whole structure, being joined together, grows into a holy temple in the Lord. In him you also are being built together into a dwelling place for God by the Spirit (Eph. 2:13-22).

Fourth, the Tabernacle of David must be restored by the Lord. This is related to Shem, Ham, and Japheth becoming one.

Blessed be the LORD, the God of Shem; and let Canaan be his servant. May God enlarge Japheth, and let him dwell in the tents of Shem, and let Canaan be his servant (Gen. 9:26-27).

According to the Genesis account, as a consequence of insolence and pride, the peoples of the earth were divided and soon deserted God. They then formed hostile relationships toward one another, evidenced by wars between nations throughout history. Unity, in the natural scheme of things, seems impossible. However, through faith in Yeshua, God has brought people of all nations into unity. This unity can be seen in the promise of the restoration of the Tabernacle of David.

> In that day I will raise up the booth of David that is fallen and repair its breaches, and raise up its ruins and rebuild it as in the days of old, that they may possess the remnant of Edom and all the nations who are called by my name," declares the LORD who does this (Am. 9:11-12).

The rebuilt booth of David will possess the remnant of Edom and all nations who are called by the Lord's name, and, as in the days of the Tabernacle of David, praises will be lifted up to the Almighty God who saves.

The descendants of Edom are the descendants of Esau. Not only will the remnant of the descendants of Esau be called by God's name, but also those of the remnant of Ishmael who will believe. Messianic Jews (Jews who believe in Yeshua), Arabic Christians (the remnant of Edom), and the international church will all become one in worship. This is already beginning to take place in Israel. The restoration of the Tabernacle of David will crown this oneness.

The Tabernacle of David will complete what needs to be fulfilled when Yeshua returns as King. The preaching of the Gospel to the ends of the earth, the spiritual restoration of Israel, and the creation of the One New Man are all connected with the Tabernacle of David. Yeshua Himself will direct the events that must be accomplished in the last days.

In the Tabernacle of David,
There is only the ark.
There is no congregation.
The Lord is the only audience.

The Incense, Prayer, and Worship of the Saints

Looking into
GOD'S WORD

Chapter 8: The Incense, Prayer, and Worship of the Saints

1. Carefully compare Revelation 5:8 and 8:3-4.

   a. In Revelation 5:8, what is the incense in the censer (the golden bowl)? In Revelation 8:3-4, what happens with the smoke of the incense and the prayers of the saints?

   b. In chapter 5, the incense that represented the prayers of the saints is different from the prayers of the saints in chapter 8. What do you think the "smoke of the incense" is?

2. Before the seven judgments are released, certain phenomena occur. Based on this, what can you infer about the incense?

   > Rev. 5:8-14; 6:1
   > Rev. 7:10-12; 8:1-6
   > Rev. 11:15-19; 15:3-8
   > Rev. 19:1-8; 19:11-16

3. We see that the incense in the golden bowl is separate from the prayers of the saints and is differentiated from the worship that follows the seven judgments in the last days. Who is offering this throne-room worship?

The Tabernacle of David is incense ascending to the throne.

The Incense, Prayer, and Worship of the Saints

WHEN WE COMPARE Revelation 5:8 and 8:3-5, we find something interesting. In Revelation Chapter 5, we see the four living creatures and the twenty-four elders with harps and golden bowls filled with incense. An explanation of what the incense represents, follows.

> And he went and took the scroll from the right hand of him who was seated on the throne. And when he had taken the scroll, the four living creatures and the twenty-four elders fell down before the Lamb, each holding a harp, and golden bowls full of incense, which are the prayers of the saints (Rev. 5:7-8).

The incense filling the golden bowl is said to be the prayers of the saints. However, in Chapter 8, the incense changes. It is separate from the prayers of the saints.

> And another angel came and stood at the altar with a golden censer, and he was given much incense to offer with the prayers of all the saints on the golden altar before the throne,

and the smoke of the incense, with the prayers of the saints, rose before God from the hand of the angel (Rev. 8:3-4).

The incense, which was previously explained as "the prayers of the saints", is now distinguished from the prayers of the saints. This raises the question: What is the "smoke of the incense" rising before the throne? It is possible to infer what that incense might be by examining the events that take place after it reaches the throne.

First, let us take a closer look at Revelation 8.

> And another angel came and stood at the altar with a golden censer, and he was given much incense to offer with the prayers of all the saints on the golden altar before the throne, and the smoke of the incense, with the prayers of the saints, rose before God from the hand of the angel. Then the angel took the censer and filled it with fire from the altar and threw it on the earth, and there were peals of thunder, rumblings, flashes of lightning, and an earthquake. Now the seven angels who had the seven trumpets prepared to blow them. The first angel blew his trumpet, and there followed hail and fire, mixed with blood, and these were thrown upon the earth. And a third of the earth was burned up, and a third of the trees were burned up, and all green grass was burned up (Rev. 8:3-7).

After the smoke of the incense rises, fire is thrown down onto the earth and the judgment of the seven trumpets begins. Revelation 11:19 is reiterated in Revelation 15:5. Similar phenomena accompany the beginning of God's seven- bowl judgment.

> The nations raged, but your wrath came, and the time for the dead to be judged, and for rewarding your servants, the prophets and saints, and those who fear your name, both small and great, and for destroying the destroyers of the earth (Rev. 11:18).

And one of the four living creatures gave to the seven angels seven golden bowls full of the wrath of God who lives forever and ever, and the sanctuary was filled with smoke from the glory of God and from his power, and no one could enter the sanctuary until the seven plagues of the seven angels were finished (Rev. 15:7-8).

Before the seven trumpets were blown and the seven bowls were poured out, the incense first ascended before the throne. The same is true of the seven seals. If we consider what happens immediately before the seven seals, the seven trumpets, the seven bowls, and the seven judgments take place, we may find a commonality and discover what the smoke of the incense might be.

Let us evaluate what occurred immediately before the seven seals were removed.

And they sang a new song, saying, 'Worthy are you to take the scroll and to open its seals, for you were slain, and by your blood you ransomed people for God from every tribe and language and people and nation, and you have made them a kingdom and priests to our God, and they shall reign on the earth.' Then I looked, and I heard around the throne and the living creatures and the elders, the voice of many angels, numbering myriads of myriads and thousands of thousands, saying with a loud voice, 'Worthy is the Lamb who was slain, to receive power and wealth and wisdom and might and honor and glory and blessing!'

And I heard every creature in heaven and on earth and under the earth and in the sea, and all that is in them, saying, 'To him who sits on the throne and to the Lamb be blessing and honor and glory and might forever and ever!'

And the four living creatures said, 'Amen!' and the elders fell down and worshipped (Rev. 5:9-14).

After the songs and proclamations of the four living creatures, the twenty-four elders, the myriads of thousands of angels, and all creatures worshipping God on their faces, He begins to break the seven seals.

Now let us look at what happens immediately before the seven trumpets are blown.

> ...and crying out with a loud voice, 'Salvation belongs to our God who sits on the throne, and to the Lamb!' And all the angels were standing around the throne and around the elders and the four living creatures, and they fell on their faces before the throne and worshipped God, saying, 'Amen! Blessing and glory and wisdom and thanksgiving and honor and power and might be to our God forever and ever! Amen (Rev. 7:10-12).

After the cry from every nation, tribe, people, and tongue, a cry from so great a multitude that no one can count, and after all the angels fall down and worship God, the seven trumpets are blown.

Let us also review what occurs immediately before the seven bowls are poured out.

> Then the seventh angel blew his trumpet, and there were loud voices in heaven, saying, 'The kingdom of the world has become the kingdom of our Lord and of his Christ, and He shall reign forever and ever.' And the twenty-four elders who sit on their thrones before God fell on their faces and worshipped God, saying, 'We give thanks to you, Lord God Almighty, who is and who was, for you have taken your great power and begun to reign. The nations raged, but your wrath came, and the time for the dead to be judged, and for rewarding your servants, the prophets and saints, and those who fear your name, both small and great, and for destroying the destroyers of the earth (Rev. 11:15-18).

And they sing the song of Moses, the servant of God, and the song of the Lamb, saying, 'Great and amazing are your deeds, O Lord God the Almighty! Just and true are your ways, O King of the nations! Who will not fear, O Lord, and glorify your name? For you alone are holy. All nations will come and worship you, for your righteous acts have been revealed' (Rev. 15:3-4).

After the Most High hears the worship of the twenty-four elders who bow down and the song of Moses and the song of the Lamb by those who have overcome, God pours out seven bowls on the ground.

What these all have in common is a song of worship. Is it possible that worship is the incense? There are surely other interpretations for what the incense might be, but we believe it is throne-room worship which opens the door to the seven judgements.

In the end times, we may see a change taking place. In addition to the prayers of the saints, throne-room worship will be offered to God by those who sing and cry out in holiness with the songs of the heavenly hosts. We believe we will see the prayers of the saints and throne-room worship developing as more separate functions.

Who will offer up this throne-room worship? Worshippers who hear the voice of the Bridegroom from heaven will offer up such worship. They will be among the watchmen awaiting the day of the Lord. This will be covered in more depth in the next chapter.

Has there been a time in the past when throne-room worship was offered to the Holy One by mortals? Has there been a worship service so heavenly and pure before the throne; worship apart from all supplications and intercessions? Most likely in the Tabernacle of David. Throne-room worship was offered at the Tabernacle of David for a time span of thirty to forty years. And we believe this throne-room worship will be restored in the end times, fulfilling, at least in part, the prophecy of Amos.

> In that day I will raise up the booth of David that is fallen and repair its breaches, and raise up its ruins and rebuild it as in the days of old (Amos 9:11, NKJV).

But the effect of this worship doesn't end with the raising of ruins. Throne-room worship is our cry for Yeshua to return and take His place as King of kings, Lord of lords, and our Heavenly Bridegroom.

> After this I heard what seemed to be the loud voice of a great multitude in heaven, crying out, 'Hallelujah! Salvation and glory and power belongs to our God, for his judgments are true and just'… Once more they cried out, 'Hallelujah!'… And the twenty-four elders and the four living creatures fell down and worshipped God…
>
> Then I heard what seemed to be the voice of a great multitude, like the roar of many waters and like the sound of mighty peals of thunder, crying out, 'Hallelujah! For the Lord our God the Almighty reigns. Let us rejoice and exult and give him the glory, for the marriage of the Lamb has come, and his Bride has made herself ready' (Rev. 19:1-7).

Yeshua will come again amidst the worship of the great crowd, the twenty-four elders, and the four living creatures.

> Then I saw heaven opened, and behold, a white horse! The one sitting on it is called Faithful and True, and in righteousness he judges and makes war (Rev. 19:11).

Yeshua is worthy of our throne-room worship. This worship, akin to the Tabernacle of David, will be restored on the earth.

The Voice Crying Out in the Wilderness and the Voices of Heaven

Looking into
GOD'S WORD

Chapter 9: The Voice Crying Out in the Wilderness and the Voices of Heaven

1. Those who prepare the way of the Lord are called, "the voice of those who cry out in the wilderness", and "watchmen" (Is. 40:3-5, 52:7-8). Who prepared the way for the first Coming of Yeshua? (Matt. 3:1-6, Jn. 3:28-30)

2. There remain watchmen who desire to prepare for the coming of King Yeshua (Is. 62:6-7). What do the watchmen most desire to shout? (Matt. 25:6, Is. 52:7)

3. In the book of Revelation, after the cry of the watchmen reaches the throne in heaven in the last days, there is a change in the subject of the cry and in those who cry out. (Rev. 1:10; 5:2; 6:1; 11:12-15; 12:10; 14:2-13; 16:17; 18:2-4; 19:1-6; 21:3).

4. The voices from heaven are expressed as the voices of angels, loud voices of a large crowd, and loud voices from the throne. In the end times, the watchmen's voice is superseded by the voice coming down from heaven. What is the response of those who hear the voice of heaven? (Rev. 5:9; 14; 11:16-17; 19:4-5)

Tabernacle of David worship is that which responds to the voice coming down from heaven.

The Voice Crying Out in the Wilderness and the Heavenly Voices

BECAUSE THEY TURNED against God, the prophet Isaiah proclaimed a message of judgment against Israel in chapters 1-39. This is followed by a message of comfort and hope, which begins in chapter 40. The voice of those who proclaim this message (40:3) and of those who preach the beautiful news (40:9, 52:7) are the watchmen (52:8, 62:6).

A voice cries: 'In the wilderness prepare the way of the LORD; make straight in the desert a highway for our God...Go on up to a high mountain, O Zion, herald of good news; lift up your voice with strength, O Jerusalem, herald of good news; lift it up, fear not; say to the cities of Judah, "Behold your God!"' (Is. 40:3,9).

How beautiful upon the mountains are the feet of him who brings good news, who publishes peace, who brings good news of happiness, who publishes salvation, who says to Zion, 'Your God reigns.' The voice of your watchmen—they lift up their voice; together they sing for joy; for eye to eye they see the return of the LORD to Zion (Is. 52:7-8).

On your walls, O Jerusalem, I have set watchmen; all the day and all the night they shall never be silent. You who put the LORD in remembrance, take no rest (Is. 62:6).

Through the cries of the watchmen, the way was prepared for the Messiah to come over 2,000 years ago. Now, the voices of the watchmen and the beautiful news which they carry, are preparing the way for the Messiah to return. John the Baptist was the last of the watchmen before Yeshua. He cried out while seeing the Messiah with his own eyes.

I myself did not know him, but for this purpose I came baptizing with water, that he might be revealed to Israel…I myself did not know him, but he who sent me to baptize with water said to me, 'He on whom you see the Spirit descend and remain, this is he who baptizes with the Holy Spirit.' And I have seen and have borne witness that this is the Son of God (Jn. 1:31, 33-34).

Yeshua, our Messiah, is the Lamb of God who took away the sins of the world by taking up His cross and being suspended upon it until death. He was then resurrected from the grave after three days. Afterwards, He taught about the kingdom of God for forty days before ascending into heaven. As He ascended, He promised to come again in the same manner in which He left (Acts 1:11). Yeshua, the One who will come again, will return as the Bridegroom for His bride (Jn. 3:29, Rev. 19:7), and the King of kings, and Lord of lords (Rev. 19:16).

The one who has the bride is the bridegroom. The friend of the bridegroom, who stands and hears him, rejoices greatly at the bridegroom's voice. Therefore, this joy of mine is now complete (Jn. 3:29).

Then I heard what seemed to be the voice of a great multitude, like the roar of many waters and like the sound of mighty peals of thunder, crying out, "Hallelujah! For the Lord our God the Almighty reigns. Let us rejoice and exult and give him the glory, for the marriage of the Lamb has come, and his Bride has made herself ready; it was granted her to clothe herself with fine linen, bright and pure"—for the fine linen is the righteous deeds of the saints (Rev. 19:6-8).

Then I saw heaven opened, and behold, a white horse! The one sitting on it is called Faithful and True, and in righteousness he judges and makes war. From his mouth comes a sharp sword with which to strike down the nations, and he will rule them with a rod of iron. He will tread the winepress of the fury of the wrath of God the Almighty. On his robe and on his thigh, he has a name written, King of kings and Lord of lords (Rev. 19:11, 15-16).

The voice of those crying out to prepare the way for Messiah, the cry of the watchmen, continues to ring out. Prepare the way for the King, our Bridegroom, to return.

On your walls, O Jerusalem, I have set watchmen; all the day and all the night they shall never be silent. You who put the LORD in remembrance, take no rest, and give him no rest until he establishes Jerusalem and makes it a praise in the earth (Is. 62:6-7).

As for me, I have set my King on Zion, my holy hill (Ps. 2:6).

My heart pounds when I think about the only words that the watchmen want to shout out. There is only one thing they await. It is to see the Messiah come for His bride. The watchman's greatest glory is to shout out: "Here is the Bridegroom!"

As the bridegroom was delayed, they all became drowsy and slept. But at midnight there was a cry, 'Here is the bridegroom! Come out to meet him.' Then all those virgins rose and trimmed their lamps (Matt. 25:5-7).

The prophet Isaiah knew that the Messiah was coming to rule. He described the cry of the one watching the Lord return to Zion as beautiful. This cry is the sound of those greeting Yeshua, the Bridegroom King.

How beautiful upon the mountains are the feet of him who brings good news, who publishes peace, who brings good news of happiness, who publishes salvation, who says to Zion, "Your God reigns." The voice of your watchmen—they lift up their voice; together they sing for joy; for eye to eye they see the return of the LORD to Zion (Is. 52:7-8).

Today, we have climbed the watchtower and are waiting to announce the coming of Yeshua, the Bridegroom. Every day, watchmen are worshipping God. This worship, differentiated from the prayers of the saints, longs to be mingled with the throne-room worship in heaven. And as it rises to the throne and becomes part of the heavenly chorus, we know that Yeshua's return is close at hand.

Until now, watchmen, prompted by the Spirit of God, were the source of their cries, but now, watchmen are replying to a sound coming down from heaven. According to the book of Revelation, in the end times, the sound does not ascend from earth but descends from heaven.

I was in the Spirit on the Lord's Day, and I heard behind me a loud voice like a trumpet (Rev. 1:10).

And I saw a mighty angel proclaiming with a loud voice, 'Who is worthy to open the scroll and break its seals?' … Then I looked, and I heard around the throne and the living creatures and the elders, the voice of many angels, numbering myriads of myriads and thousands of thousands, saying with a loud voice, 'Worthy is the Lamb who was slain, to receive power and wealth and wisdom and might and honor and glory and blessing!' (Rev. 5:2, 11-12).

And I heard a loud voice in heaven, saying, 'Now the salvation and the power and the kingdom of our God and the authority of his Christ have come, for the accuser of our brothers has been thrown down, who accuses them day and night before our God' (Rev. 12:10).

And I heard a voice from heaven like the roar of many waters and like the sound of loud thunder. The voice I heard was like the sound of harpists playing on their harps... And he said with a loud voice, 'Fear God and give him glory, because the hour of his judgment has come, and worship him who made heaven and earth, the sea and the springs of water' ... And another angel, a third, followed them, saying with a loud voice, 'If anyone worships the beast and its image and receives a mark on his forehead or on his hand'...And I heard a voice from heaven saying, 'Write this: Blessed are the dead who die in the Lord from now on.' 'Blessed indeed,' says the Spirit, 'that they may rest from their labors, for their deeds follow them!' (Rev. 14:2,7,9,13).

The seventh angel poured out his bowl into the air, and a loud voice came out of the temple, from the throne, saying, 'It is Done!' (Rev. 16:17).

And he called out with a mighty voice, 'Fallen, fallen is Babylon the great! She has become a dwelling place for demons, a haunt for every unclean spirit, a haunt for every unclean bird, a haunt for every unclean and detestable beast'... Then I heard another voice from heaven saying, 'Come out of her, my people, lest you take part in her sins, lest you share in her plagues' (Rev. 18:2,4).

After this I heard what seemed to be the loud voice of a great multitude in heaven, crying out, 'Hallelujah! Salvation and glory and power belong to our God'… And from the throne came a voice saying, 'Praise our God, all you his servants, you who fear him, small and great.' Then I heard what seemed to be the voice of a great multitude, like the roar of many waters and like the sound of mighty peals of thunder, crying out, 'Hallelujah! For the Lord our God the Almighty reigns' (Rev. 19:1, 5-6).

And I heard a loud voice from the throne saying, 'Behold, the dwelling place of God is with man. He will dwell with them, and they will be his people, and God himself will be with them as their God' (Rev. 21:3).

These Scriptures signify the voice coming down from heaven. Accordingly, as watchmen, we shift from the position of one crying out to one responding to the voice from heaven. As we hear this sound descending, we answer with throne-room worship. We are inwardly compelled to bow down and worship with a new song, worshipping before the throne in spirit and in truth.

And they sang a new song, saying, 'Worthy are you to take the scroll and to open its seals, for you were slain, and by your blood you ransomed people for God from every tribe and language and people and nation, and you have made them a kingdom and priests to our God, and they shall reign on the earth.' Then I looked, and I heard around the throne and the living creatures and the elders the voice of many angels, numbering myriads of myriads and thousands of thousands, saying with a loud voice, 'Worthy is the Lamb who was slain, to receive power and wealth and wisdom and might and honor and glory and blessing!' And I heard every creature in heaven and on earth and under the earth and in the sea, and all that is in them, saying, 'To him who sits on the throne and to the Lamb be blessing and honor and glory and might forever and Ever!' And the four living creatures said, 'Amen!' and the elders fell down and worshipped (Rev. 5:9-14).

And the twenty-four elders who sit on their thrones before God fell on their faces and worshipped God, saying, 'We give thanks to you, Lord God Almighty, who is and who was, for you have taken your great power and begun to reign' (Rev. 11:16-17).

And the twenty-four elders and the four living creatures fell down and worshipped God who was seated on the throne, saying, 'Amen. Hallelujah!' And from the throne came a voice saying, 'Praise our God, all you his servants, you who fear him, small and great' (Rev. 19:4-5).

Yeshua ascended to heaven declaring that He would come again. Over the past two thousand years, the same cry as that of John the Baptist has continued until this day. And the watchmen who once cried out are now responding to the voice of heaven and are worshipping.

As the end of this era approaches, may the restoration of the worship of the Tabernacle of David take place, for it is the LORD who will repair, raise up and rebuild this Tabernacle.

'In that day I will raise up the booth of David that is fallen and repair its breaches, and raise up its ruins and rebuild it as in the days of old, that they may possess the remnant of Edom and all the nations who are called by my name', declares the LORD who does this (Am. 9:11-12).

As Israel is restored, we believe she will increasingly participate in worship like unto that of the Tabernacle of David. Until now, the nations were preeminent in worship, but today the Jews, the remnant of Edom, and the nations are worshipping together as prophesied in the book of Amos. The worship coming from this One New Man has begun to appear in the body of believers in Yeshua.

Practical Worship in the Tabernacle of David, Part I

Looking into
GOD'S WORD

Chapter 10: Practical Worship in the Tabernacle of David, Part I

1. The Tabernacle of David is where heaven's worship can be reflected on earth. It is worship before the throne of the glory of God (Rev. 4-5; 1 Chron. 25). If we desire to worship the way it was done in the Tabernacle of David, what changes must occur in the way we currently worship?

2. In heavenly worship, one cannot offer praise that ultimately seeks one's own benefit, there are no pleas for help, there is no intercession. In the Holy of Holies, only the purest worship and adoration of the King is present (Is. 6:1-5; Rev. 4:8-11, 5:9-14, 7:10-12, 19:1-8).

3. One mustn't be satisfied with the confession of one's lips, but must accompany confession with action (Rev. 7:11, 11:17-18).

4. The Tabernacle of David is 24-hour, perpetual worship that aims to be akin to that of the four living creatures and twenty-four elders before the throne in heaven (Rev. 4:8, 1 Chron. 25, Is. 62:6-7).

The worship of the Tabernacle of David is an authentic, continual offering before the King of kings.

Practical Worship in the Tabernacle of David, Part I

THE WORSHIP OFFERED in the Tabernacle of David is worship which seeks to echo that found in the Holy of Holies. There is no congregation before whom this worship is offered, it is not for the sake of a congregation. This worship is directed to One only, and after a manner consistent with what the Most High receives in heaven.

The Holy of Holies is the place where the glory of God dwells. Therefore, there can be no praise for the ears of others, no pride, no pleas, nor intercessions that seek personal benefits. It is not the time nor the place for focusing on our own consolation, encouragement, or personal hopes. It is not when we pray for ministries, missions, or crisis situations. It is where we sing praises to God declaring His holy character and beauty. In the midst of this exclusive worship, we can only seek what He desires.

When we look at what is declared in the Holy of Holies in Heaven, we find that everything focuses on God the Father and Yeshua the King.

> In the year that King Uzziah died I saw the Lord sitting upon a throne, high and lifted up; and the train of his robe filled the

temple. Above him stood the seraphim. Each had six wings: with two he covered his face, and with two he covered his feet, and with two he flew. And one called to another and said: 'Holy, holy, holy is the LORD of hosts; the whole earth is full of his Glory!' (Is. 6:1-3).

And the four living creatures, each of them with six wings, are full of eyes all around and within, and day and night they never cease to say, 'Holy, holy, holy, is the Lord God Almighty, who was and is and is to come!' And whenever the living creatures give glory and honor and thanks to him who is seated on the throne, who lives forever and ever, the twenty-four elders fall down before him who is seated on the throne and worship him who lives forever and ever. They cast their crowns before the throne, saying, 'Worthy are you, our Lord and God, to receive glory and honor and power, for you created all things, and by your will they existed and were created' (Rev. 4:8-11).

The praises of the seraphim, the four living creatures, and the twenty-four elders are solely directed toward the holiness and essence of God who sits on the throne. It is pure exaltation.

It follows that actions should accompany these declarations of praise to the Almighty.

> …the twenty-four elders fall down before him who is seated on the throne and worship him who lives forever and ever. They cast their crowns before the throne… (Rev. 4:10)

> And the twenty-four elders who sit on their thrones before God fell on their faces and worshipped God, saying, 'We give thanks to you, Lord God Almighty, who is and who was, for you have taken your great power and begun to reign' (Rev. 11:16-17).

The twenty-four elders cannot limit themselves to vocal praise. The confession of their lips is accompanied by an irresistible impulse to fall on their faces before God. Our posture should also reflect our words and the holiness of the One before whom we offer praise. True worship is to properly honor the King of kings.

Not long ago in Korea, we knelt down and prostrated ourselves before the king. I remember it vividly even now.

During Hannukah, December 12, 2015, we were worshipping the Lord and suddenly God asked me,

"Who am I?"

"Lord, you are King."

"If you consider me the King, then come with the proper reverence."

We paused our worship as I shared God's message. We then continued our worship prostrated before Him. This was a turning point for us as we grew in our understanding of what it meant to worship the King. Now, it is very natural for us to prostrate ourselves whenever we worship the King.

Just as the four living creatures and the twenty-four elders worship before the throne day and night without ceasing, the Tabernacle of David is a place of 24-hour worship. David arranged the worship with all appointed Levites who were well-trained in singing and playing musical instruments. These Levites were divided into twenty-four teams that alternated for day and night worship. God deserves uninterrupted worship that continues day and night.

> And the four living creatures, each of them with six wings, are full of eyes all around and within, and day and night they never cease to say, 'Holy, holy, holy, is the Lord God Almighty, who was and is and is to come!' (Rev. 4:8).

> On your walls, O Jerusalem, I have set watchmen; all the day and all the night they shall never be silent. You who put the

LORD in remembrance, take no rest, and give him no rest until he establishes Jerusalem and makes it a praise in the earth (Is. 62:6-7).

Our manner of worship is according to our understanding and experience of God. At the Tabernacle of Moses, they worshipped the covenant-keeping, merciful God. At the Tabernacle of David, they worshipped the King who governs the Kingdom of God and His servant Israel. We worship Yeshua the Savior who has redeemed us, the covenant-keeping, merciful God, and the King of kings who is coming to rule and reign in righteousness forever.

The worship of the Tabernacle of David is faithfully worshipping King Yeshua, reverently, in a manner befitting His holiness.

Practical Worship in the Tabernacle of David, Part II

Looking into
GOD'S WORD

Chapter 11: Practical Worship in the Tabernacle of David, Part II

1. In Tabernacle of David worship, the Holy Spirit leads the worship of God the Father and His Son, Yeshua (Jn. 4:23-24, 2 Tim. 3:16, 1 Cor. 2:10).

2. The worship of the Tabernacle of David is not offered according to our plans, ideas, or decisions. It is a matter of obedience to the King alone (Pr. 19:21, Ps. 33:10-11, Matt. 8:8-9).

3. In Tabernacle of David worship, we sing new songs according to what the King desires (Ps. 47:7, Rev. 5:9, Ps. 40:3).

If all worshipped in the manner of the Tabernacle of David, what changes would result?

We do not lead worship in the Tabernacle of David.

Practical Worship in the Tabernacle of David, Part II

IN TABERNACLE OF David worship, there is no director of worship leading a congregation. Worship is led by the Holy Spirit. At the Holy Spirit's leading, worship is given to our Father God and King Yeshua. Yeshua spoke of those who would worship in Spirit and in Truth.

> But the hour is coming, and is now here, when the true worshippers will worship the Father in spirit and truth, for the Father is seeking such people to worship him. God is spirit, and those who worship him must worship in spirit and truth (Jn. 4:23-24).

The only way to know the mind of God is through the Spirit of God. If the Spirit of God is not leading us, then we cannot give God the worship that He desires or deserves.

> …these things God has revealed to us through the Spirit. For the Spirit searches everything, even the depths of God. For who knows a person's thoughts except the spirit of that person, which is in him? So also no one comprehends the thoughts of God except the Spirit of God (1 Cor. 2:10-11).

The Bible, inspired by the Holy Spirit, is used in Tabernacle of David worship. When we worship with the Word, the Holy Spirit reveals the heart of God to us.

> All Scripture is breathed out by God and profitable for teaching, for reproof, for correction, and for training in righteousness (2 Tim. 3:16).

In Tabernacle of David worship, we serve as watchmen who watch and worship together with praises that originate with creating melodies to accompany God's Holy Scripture.

We sing the Word of God in adoration. Even if the melody is incomplete, we begin to sing the Word, and as we sing, tunes begin to develop. Each can sing the Word according to the tune with which he is inspired by the Holy Spirit. Because the Word is a love story, it can be more beautiful when sung than when spoken. God enjoys our sincere songs of praise.

At the Tabernacle of David, we sing only what we believe the King desires to hear. We follow no formulas, only what He puts in our hearts as we worship. This sometimes means that the only way to proceed is to allow Him to create the song through us. This is how we sing a new song—it is the birth of the King's song.

Because Tabernacle of David worship is not something we enter into according to our own plans, we relinquish the power of decision over the order of worship. This is because we know our thoughts and God's thoughts are vastly different from each other.

> 'For my thoughts are not your thoughts, neither are your ways my ways', declares the LORD. 'For as the heavens are higher than the earth, so are my ways higher than your ways and my thoughts than your thoughts. For as the rain and the snow come down from heaven and do not return there but water the earth, making it bring forth and sprout, giving seed to the

sower and bread to the eater, so shall my word be that goes out from my mouth; it shall not return to me empty, but it shall accomplish that which I purpose, and shall succeed in the thing for which I sent it' (Is. 55:8-11).

No matter how correct we may regard our own ideas and intentions to be, they may be far from the King's thoughts. And upon surrendering our will and plans, we discover that God's will and His master plan will last forever.

> Many are the plans in the mind of a man, but it is the purpose of the LORD that will stand (Pr. 19:21).

In this worship, there is only obedience; when the King calls us to worship, we worship. Nothing is greater or more important than obeying the King.

> But the centurion replied, 'Lord, I am not worthy to have you come under my roof, but only say the word, and my servant will be healed. For I too am a man under authority, with soldiers under me. And I say to one, "Go," and he goes, and to another, "Come," and he comes, and to my servant, "Do this," and he does it' (Matt. 8:8-9).

Because Tabernacle of David worship is that in which all thoughts, plans, and decisions belong to the King, we immerse ourselves in His Word to know His thoughts, and to understand His plans, and to honor His decisions. And we continue to worship with hearts willing to experiment, learn and grow. We consider what we can do to go deeper into reverent awe as we worship God, desiring always to worship Him in the beauty of holiness.

One day He said to me: "What kind of musical instruments do you use when the king's processional passes before you?"

So, we procured the instruments that are used in the king's processional in Korea and began to experiment and worship with those musical instruments: *buk* (traditional barrel-shaped Korean drum), *janggu* (Korean double-headed drum), *kkwaenggwari* (a small gong), *jing* (large gong), *jabara* (large brass cymbals), flags and banners. We endeavor to discover what pleases the Most High and worship Him accordingly. This is how He has led us. How will He lead you?

Let us exalt His name together and grow deeper into the purity and veneration of worshipping the Holy One. King Yeshua is worthy.

Persevering Until the Coming of Yeshua

The Tabernacle of David,
where only the Lord is revered,
there is throne-room worship.

Persevering Until the Coming of Yeshua

WE ALREADY KNOW. We can sense that the day is drawing near. The day when the kingdoms of this world will be subdued and the reign of God's Kingdom will begin on earth.

And the LORD will be king over all the earth. On that day the LORD will be one and his name one (Zech. 14:9).

As that day approaches, Satan will increase his activities to divide, deceive, and destroy all he can, all over the earth.

> 'Therefore, rejoice, O heavens and you who dwell in them! But woe to you, O earth and sea, for the devil has come down to you in great wrath, because he knows that his time is short!' And when the dragon saw that he had been thrown down to the earth, he pursued the woman who had given birth to the male child (Rev. 12:12-13).

However, the Lord of lords and King of kings will return to Jerusalem, and He will strike the nations with an iron rod.

> Then I saw heaven opened, and behold, a white horse! The one sitting on it is called Faithful and True, and in righteousness he judges and makes war (Rev. 19:11).

Yeshua, the King of kings and Lord of lords, is worthy to receive all praise. Satan has done his utmost to usurp the worship that belongs to the Lord God Almighty, King Yeshua. As that day approaches, the battle over whom we will worship will intensify. Satan will masquerade himself as the Messiah. The only way to win in this war of deception is to cling to the Almighty through prayer, through His Word, and through worshipping Him wholeheartedly as the King, the only One who is worthy of our obedience, devotion and praise.

God is raising up the Tabernacle of David, the place where He once received sanctified, reverential, uninterrupted worship. We know of nothing else like it in human history. Worship like unto that of Heaven's Holy of Holies, worship that can only be given to the King of the universe, is now being restored. Through Tabernacle of David worship, we proclaim to all the nations the One who is worthy of all praise. Worship that is pure ascends to the throne of God.

> And another angel came and stood at the altar with a golden censer, and he was given much incense to offer with the prayers of all the saints on the golden altar before the throne, and the smoke of the incense, with the prayers of the saints, rose before God from the hand of the angel. Then the angel took the censer and filled it with fire from the altar and threw it on the earth, and there were peals of thunder, rumblings, flashes of lightning, and an earthquake. Now the seven angels who had the seven trumpets prepared to blow them (Rev. 8:3-6).

When the incense from the golden censers rises to God before His throne, it will usher in the day of the coming of King Yeshua. The Tabernacle of David will offer worship until the day King Yeshua returns.

> In that day I will raise up the booth of David that is fallen and repair its breaches, and raise up its ruins and rebuild it as in the days of old (Amos 9:11, NKJV).

We earnestly desire to see the Tabernacle of David rising again. God promised that He would raise up the fallen Tabernacle of David on that day. This is not merely symbolic language. Let us not be satisfied with the worship in which we've participated in the past. Instead, let us press on to see Tabernacle of David worship return in all of its glory to the King. This is the time. As we read in Acts 15, the Gentile nations are ready. Furthermore, Messianic Jews are also entering into this worship. The united worship rising from the One New Man of both Jews and Gentiles is a reality. Let us come together with one heart and one mind to offer Tabernacle of David worship to our King.

During Pentecost in 2018, we went to Mt. Carmel after worshipping at the Jerusalem House of Prayer for All Nations. After being introduced to Kehilat HaCarmel Prayer Cave, we requested and received permission to worship there. As we were worshipping, God revealed His instruction to worship 24-hours, day and night, beginning with the Feast of Trumpets and ending with Yom Kippur (the Day of Atonement). In addition, God put on our hearts to prepare in advance for thirty days for this ten-day period of worship. In total, we worshipped and prayed for forty days with a heart of *Teshuvah* (הבושת) at the Kehilat HaCarmel Prayer Cave. (*Teshuvah* means "repentance, turning around." It is a 40-day fast and prayer time, which Moses did after he broke the first stone tablets which he received at Mt. Sinai in response to the golden calf and idol worship, and before he received the second tablets. We call these 40 days Teshuvah, and it lasts from Av 30 to Tishrei 10, the Day of Atonement.)

For ten days, from the Feast of Trumpets to the Day of Atonement, we especially worshipped day and night, 24-hours a day. On the eighteenth day of the forty days, God posed to us the following question: "Could you offer up Tabernacle of David worship here, day and night, 24 hours a day, without ceasing?"

"Yes! Lord! We will do it to the best of our ability."

We answered Him by worshipping 24 hours, day and night, beginning with the Feast of First Fruits on April 21, 2019. On this day, we received the encouragement and prayer of the Kehilat HaCarmel leadership.

God has been performing miracles that only He can accomplish. Through the worship of watchmen, heaven's doors are opening so that the nations can worship 24 hours a day.

We believe God will send countless Jewish worshippers as well as worshippers from the nations to the Tabernacle of David. We yearn to see the worship that has begun on Mt. Carmel flourish and disseminate all over the world, fulfilling God's promise of raising up the fallen Tabernacle of David.

The restoration of the Tabernacle of David is not our idea. It is God's idea. And as such, it will surely come to pass. We can imagine it; we have tasted it. Many worshippers from among the nations desire to participate in this worship on Mount Carmel and in other locations and nations. We dream of worshipping day and night together with dozens or even hundreds of others, divided into 24 teams, as in the time of David.

Tabernacle of David worship will not cease until the day that King Yeshua comes again to rule and reign.

May it please our Father to use us as instruments for this work.

Bibliography

Baxter Jr., Irvin. "Evidence That Now Is the End of The Age." Brad TV. May 9, 2018. Video, 36:52. https://youtu.be/Jxho9UCWUzE

"In that day I will raise up
the booth of David that is fallen
and repair its breaches,
and raise up its ruins
and rebuild it as in the days of old,
that they may possess the remnant of Edom
and all the nations who are called by my name,"
declares the LORD who does this.

Amos 9:11-12 (NKJV)

Translator's Notes

It has been an honor and a blessing to be part of the translation team for this book, which contains precious revelations of the Father's heart and exalts King Yeshua! I am so thankful for Pastor Kim and the KOG family—for their absolute devotion and obedience to the King. May this book contribute to the raising up of watchmen and worshippers for the Tabernacle of David. In worship and prayer, may we eagerly and with hope await the day of Yeshua's return and His Kingdom reign. May the Lamb of God receive the full reward of His suffering!

JANET JUN

To my Editor Cathy Smith

I would like to express my sincere gratitude to Cathy who is a very attentive and exceptional editor. It is an honor for me to have worked with her. Cathy's love and respect for the Word of God is truly inspiring. I pray God will touch you deeply for the help you have given to this book.

Afterword

THIS BOOK IS a revised edition which is being released in English first. I had thought that it would be impossible to translate into English, but Janet Jun read my book and was so moved that she volunteered to translate it. I would like to thank her again.

After the translation, it also had to be proofread. Aaron and Mary Downs are very precious friends that we met on Mount Carmel. They regarded this as their own book and guided the whole process to make it possible to publish it. They introduced me to their precious friend Cathy Smith who did the editing. I am so grateful for the work of Aaron and Mary Downs and especially Cathy.

I would also like to thank the Easterngate team in New Jersey. This whole team provided feedback while studying with my book and helped me in many ways. I would like to thank the Kehilat leadership for allowing our team to worship at the Elijah Prayer Cave in Kehilat Hacarmel for two years. Thank you!

Also, to Sharbel and Wendy Halloun from One New Man House on Mount Carmel and all our family there. And Pastor Glenn and Coralie Rowbotham from the Elohim House of Prayer together with everyone we met on Mount Carmel. Thank you, Everyone!

This book began with the worship offered up by the KOG Tabernacle of David family. I am deeply grateful that we have walked together for more than ten years on a path untraveled. Though we didn't understand, we worshipped, and worshipped, and then we worshipped more.

Above all thank you to those who were there in the beginning, when there was little light, but who steadfastly kept watch in silence: Yujin Lee, Grace Jeong, Anna Noh.

To those families in our community who came daily after work hours for nightly worship and kept their night watches these past ten years: Hyunyoung Ju and family (John Lee, Jaeah); Sungjun Kim and family (Heejin Song, Joice, Hayoung); Incheol Yeom and family (Huia Kim, Seonjae, Sanguk, Hawon); Keojang Na and family (Sunhee Kim, Sunyul, Rayul, Raim); Hannah Kim, Mrs. Geumju Kim.

Also, to the Tabernacle of David families who have walked this path together, and to all those who have walked this path, strengthened us, and then returned home to their inheritance, thank you all.

And finally, to my beloved wife Gloria Choi, who graciously said "Yes." to living her entire life with a man who is just a tent keeper, and to my beloved children, Sophia and Yoel.

May this book offer you some encouragement.

KOG Tabernacle of David's Tent-Keeper